Hector
the
Misunderstood
Snake

by Kimberly K. Schmidt

Illustrated by Marina Saumell

Library of Congress Control Number: 2020925484
ISBN: 978-0-9864009-3-3

Published by Barnyard Press
USA

Illustrated by Marina Saumell
www.marimell.com

To my boys, Taylor and Parker,
and all the pet snakes they've had
through the years.

3

GRAYSON FARM

Fox Den

Big Barn

Duck Pond

Henry's Pen

Farmhouse

Cow Field

Dairy Barn

Hen House

Hector was enjoying sunning himself in the barnyard when he was startled awake.

"EEK! It's a snake!" the children shrieked.
"Keep away. Watch out!" shouted a woman, pointing at Hector.
"Snakes are sneaky and slimy. They're poisonous!"

Hector's glossy black scales shone in the sun. He looked around to see what the shouting was about.

"Oh. They're afraid of *me*," he said sadly.

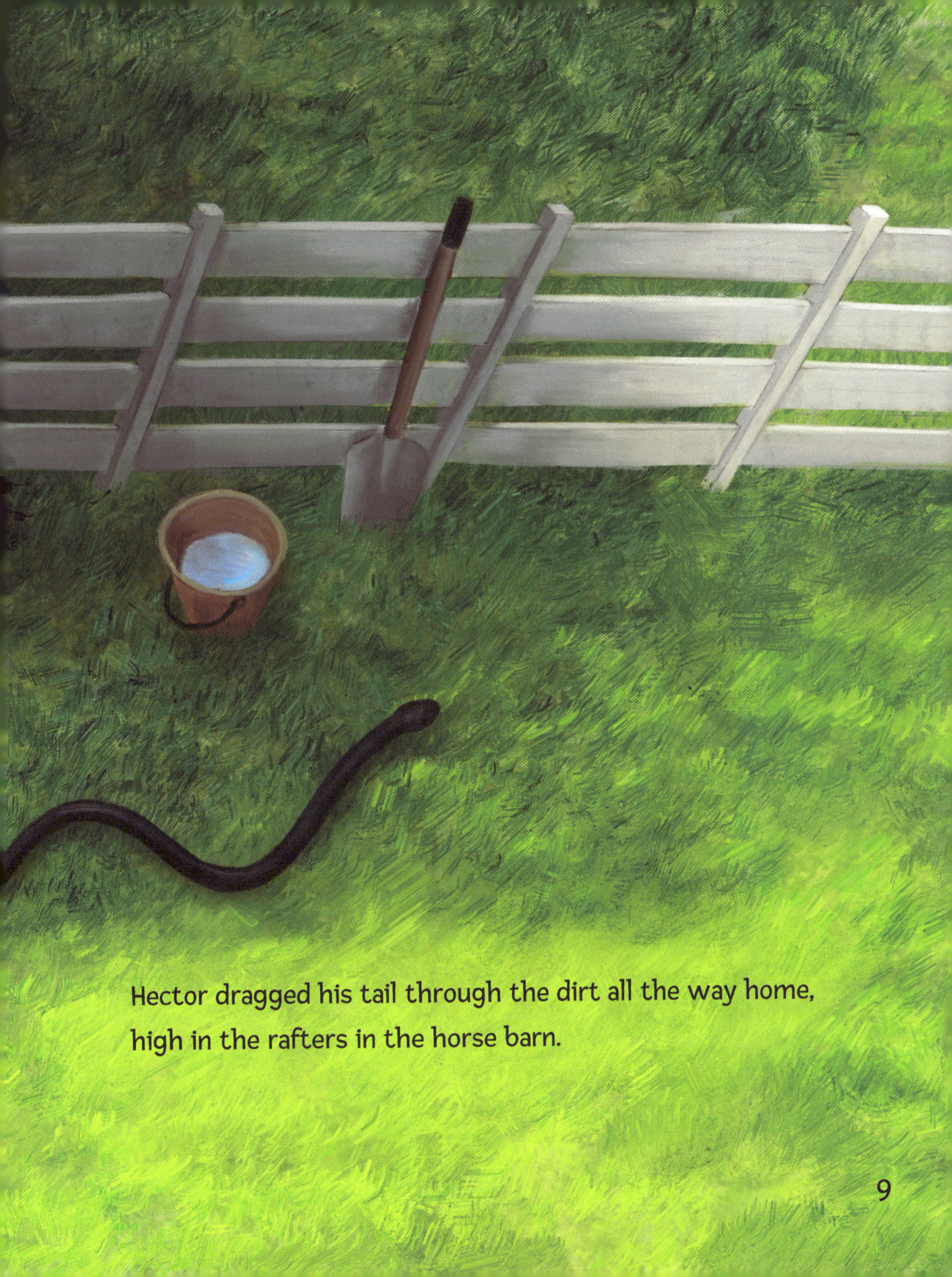

Hector dragged his tail through the dirt all the way home, high in the rafters in the horse barn.

"Mother, why do children and animals run from me whenever they see me?"

"It's because you're a snake," she said gently.

"But I'm not sneaky or slimy or poisonous. Why did that lady say those mean things?"

10

"She's afraid and doesn't
know better," Mother said.
"But why?"
"Hector, are you a good boy?"
"Yes, most of the time."
"Are you polite to others?"
"Yes, I think so."
"Are you nice to others?"
"Yes, I try to be."
"Well then, that's all you can do. You can't change others.
All you can do is be yourself."

"I wish I had a friend," sighed Hector as he slid across the barnyard.

"Watch out!" said Mrs. Little as she skidded to a stop in her pickup truck. "I almost ran over you."

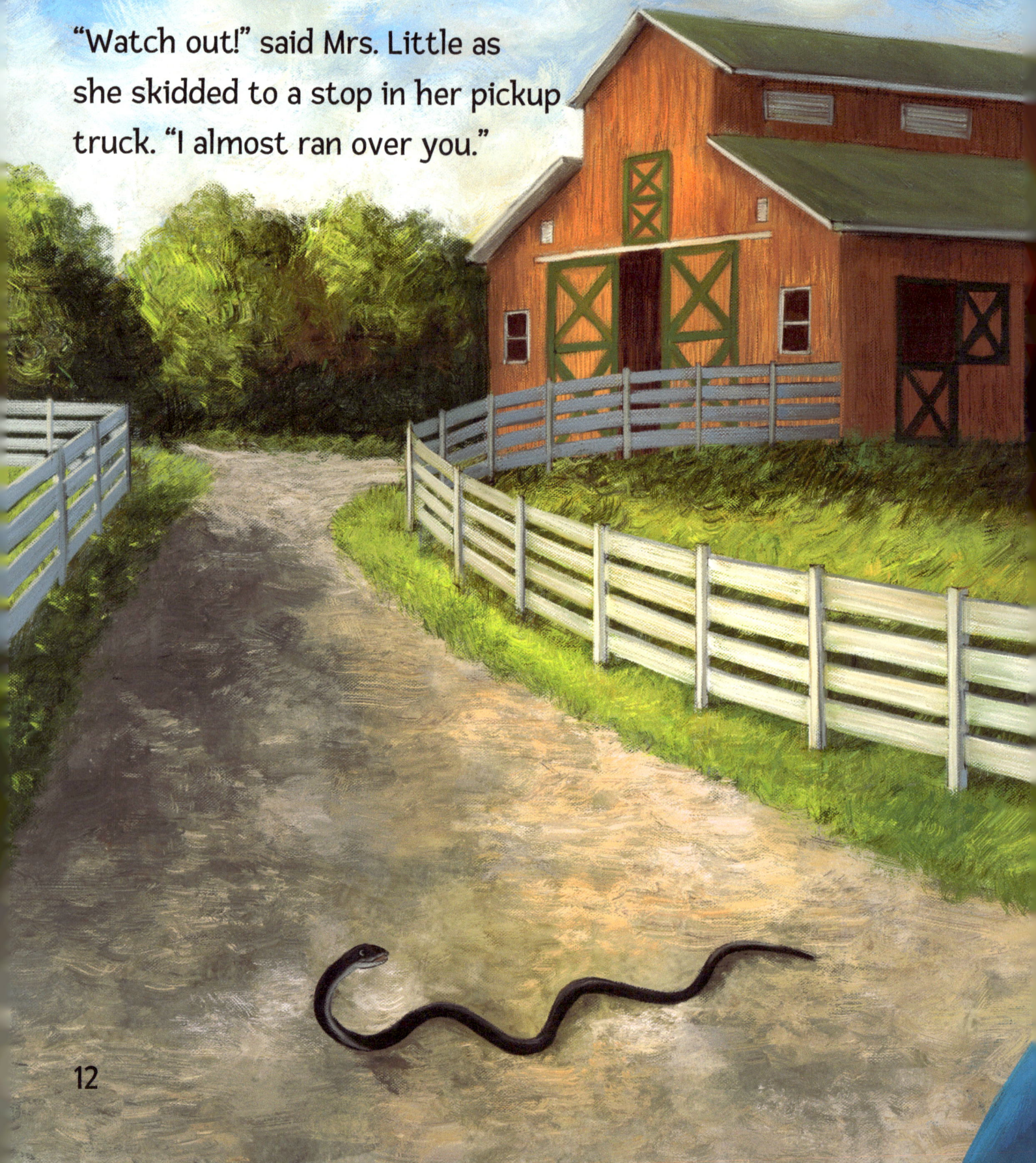

Mrs. Little liked black snakes because they kept the mouse population down. The mice chewed holes in the feed bags and made a mess.

"Be more careful now." She shook her head and smiled at Hector.

Hector was a good climber. He climbed high up into a big tree overlooking all the animals in the barnyard.

"I'm different from the other animals. I don't have fur or legs, and I don't bark or cluck or meow.
I wish I was like them," said Hector. "Then they'd like me."
Hector thought and thought. Then he had an idea.

"I know what I'll do," he said.

Hector rolled in the mud and then in the chicken feathers so they stuck to him. "Now they'll think I'm a chicken, and they'll like me."

"Hi. My name is Hector. Will you be my friend?" Hector asked the chicks.
"Haha!" The chicks laughed. "You look funny. And you're dirty. Haha!"

Hector tried again. He found an old bone and carried it around, pretending to chew on it. "Yuck!"

"My name is Hector. Will you be my friend?"

"Grrr." The farm dogs growled and circled him. "Give us back our bone, Snake. You don't fool us."

Hector dropped the bone. He slid home to the rafters in the horse barn. His mother tucked him into bed extra tenderly that night.

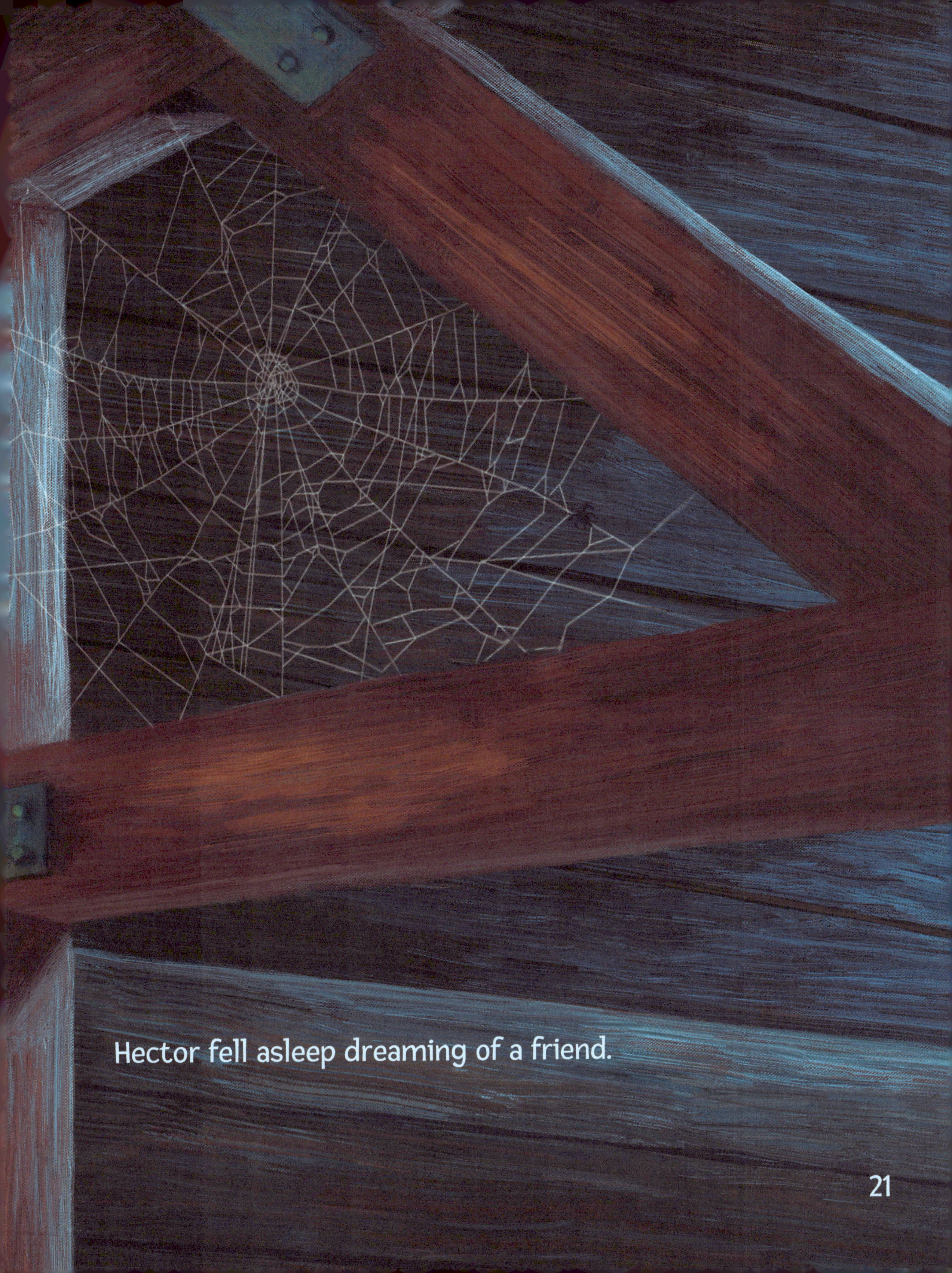

Hector fell asleep dreaming of a friend.

The next day Hector saw a truck pulling a trailer
up the drive with something large and strange.
"What is that, Mother?"

"That's a boat. I've heard of them.
They float on large lakes called oceans."

Hector was curious about this new thing.
He slithered around the corner and looked at the huge boat.
"Wow!"

Something moved. It had brown fur, a pointy face, small beady eyes, and a long bald tail.

"I wish I had a friend.
I wonder if this animal will be my friend."

The animal looked at him,
lips curled back and
yellow teeth flashing.

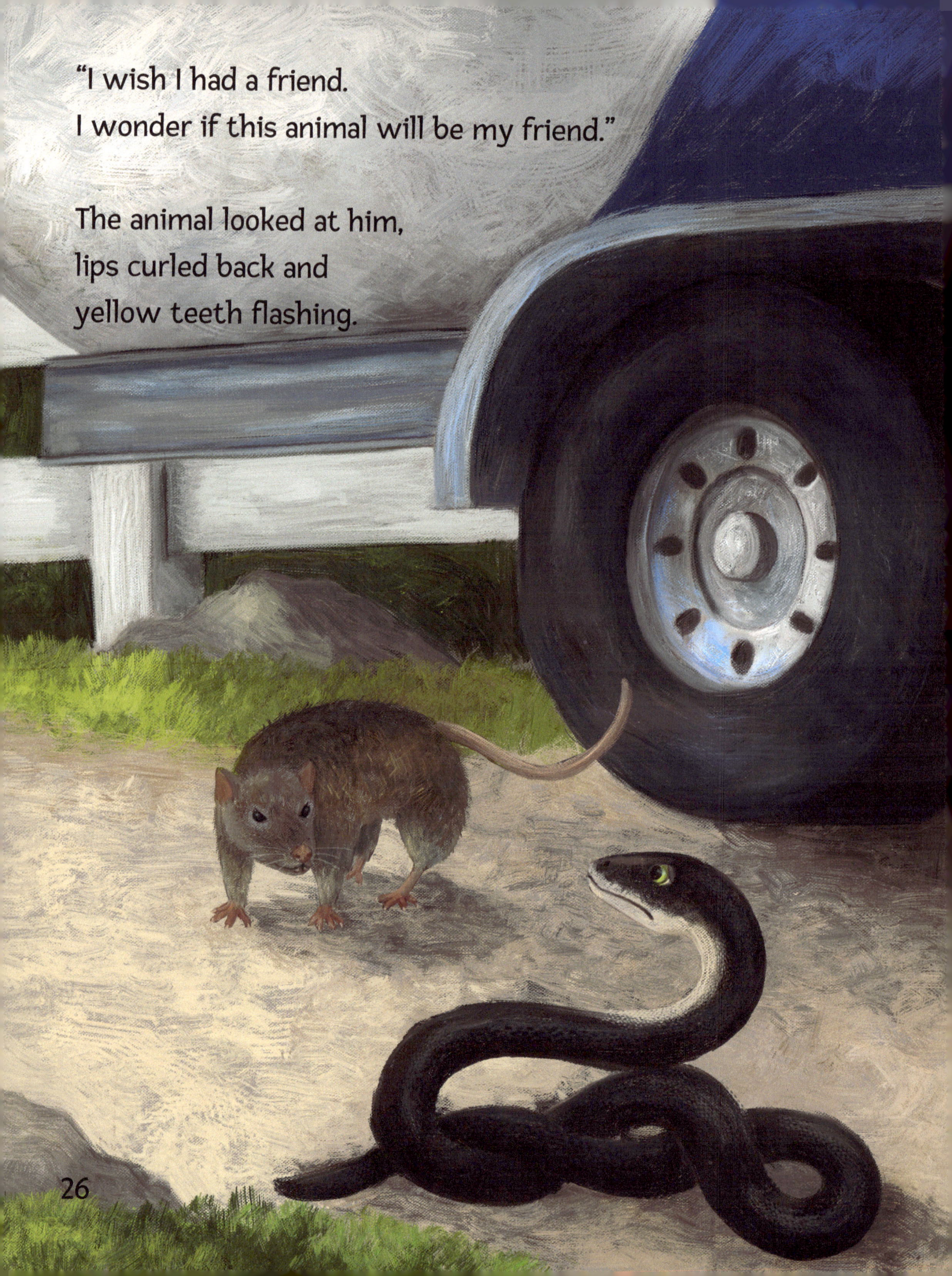

Hector rushed home to tell his
mother about the new animal on the boat.

"What was it, Mother?"
Mother frowned. "It was probably a big rat.
Mrs. Little won't like rats on her farm."

27

The next morning Hector was awakened by loud noises.

"Squawk, squawk! Cluck, cluck!"
Hector hurried over to the henhouse to see why the chickens were upset.

There was the rat, lips pulled back and teeth flashing.
Mama Hen squawked and flapped her wings,
trying to scare the rat away.

Sergeant Pepper, the big rooster, charged the rat and scratched him with his long toenails.

"Ouch!" the rat said in a low, growly voice.
"I'll be back. You'll be sorry."
He looked at them sideways and slunk away.

"Calm down, children. He's gone. Come here under my wings," said Mama Hen.

She saw Hector watching. "Oh! You snake. Go away!" She held her chicks close.

"I wish I had a friend," said Hector.

Then he saw the rat. It slunk through the open feed room door. He knew that Puzzle, the mother cat, and her kittens were nestled in the corner.

"Hiss! Mrrrow!" Puzzle hissed and growled.

Hector, silent as only a snake can be, sneaked up
behind the rat. He curled his body into a coiled spring.
As the rat moved to snatch a kitten, Hector struck.

He grabbed the rat with his open mouth and quickly
wrapped his body around it, squeezing tightly.
He held onto the struggling rat and waited.
Then he unwound his coils.

The rat, exhausted, took deep breaths and dragged
himself away from Hector.

"Go away, rat, and never come back," said Hector firmly.

The rat slunk toward the door, giving Hector a wide berth. "I'm going back to my boat and the ocean where there are no snakes," he said as he skulked away.

"Oh, my!" said Mrs. Little, who walked into the feed room just as the huge rat slipped past her and Hector finished uncoiling.

"Hector, you're a good snake!" she said. "You saved my chicks and kittens."

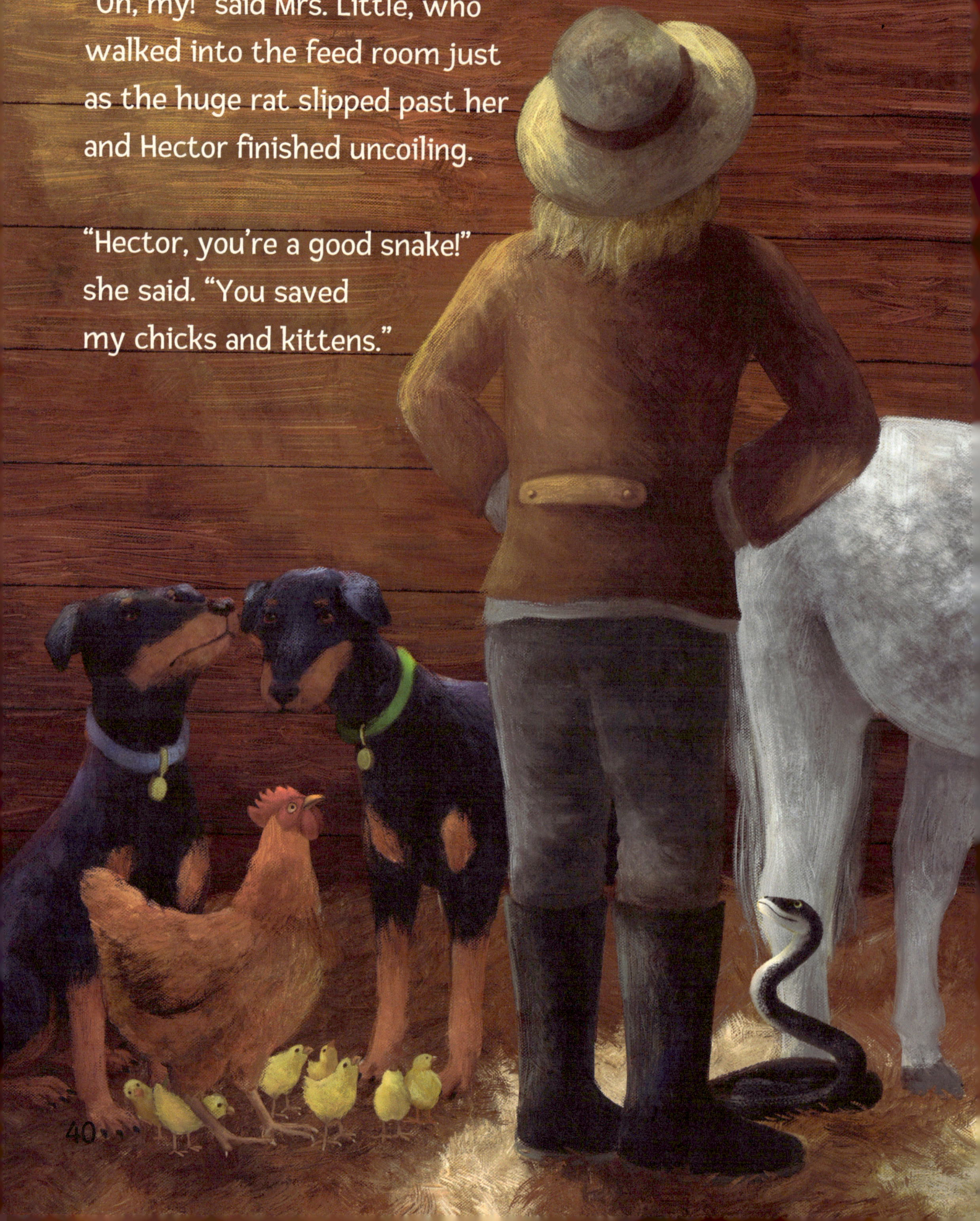

Puzzle and Mama Hen gathered their babies.

Hands on her hips, Mrs. Little looked around, peering over her glasses sternly at the animals who had hurried into the barnyard after hearing all the commotion.

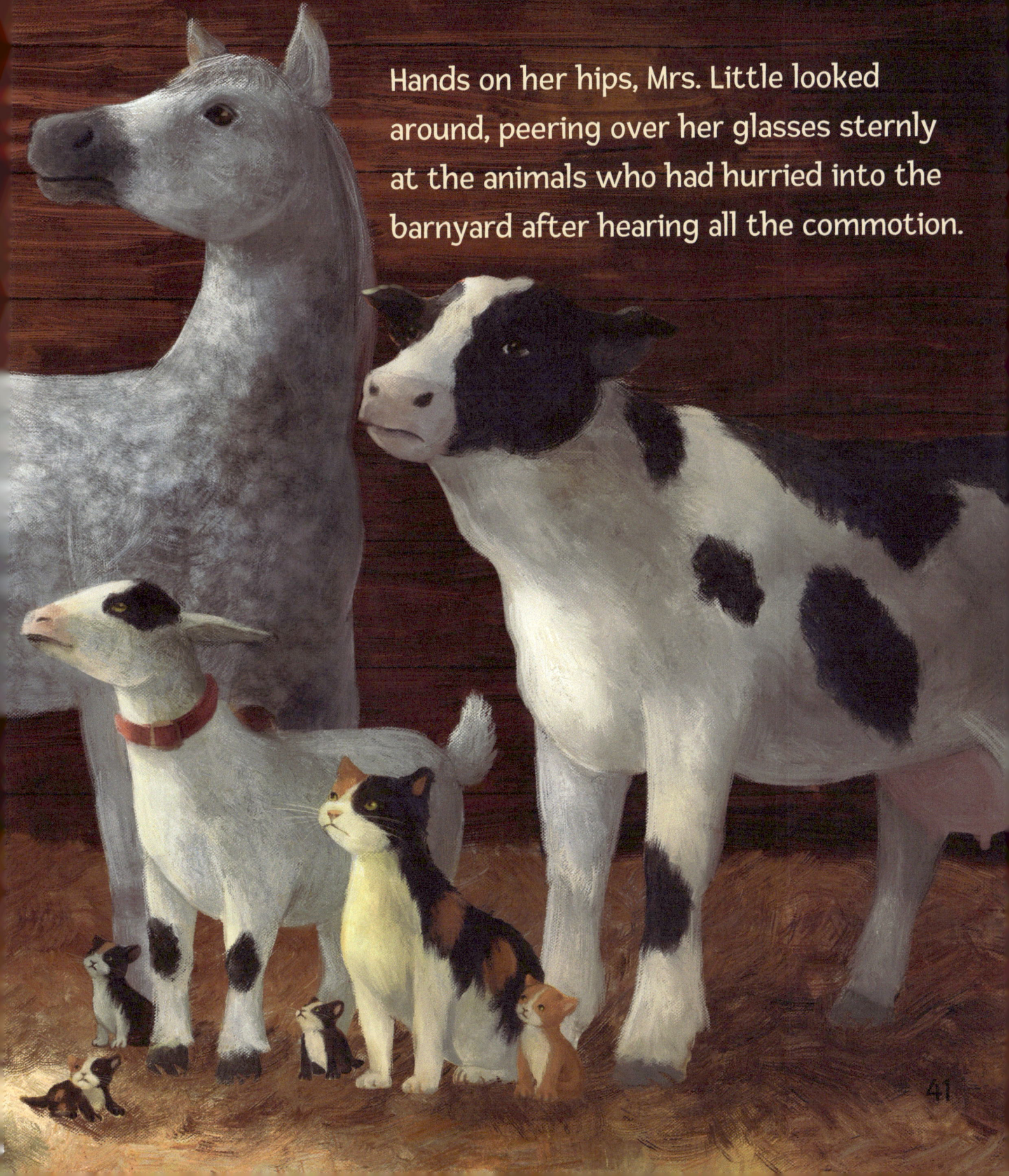

41

"I hope you have all learned from this," said Mrs. Little. "Don't be afraid of something just because you don't know it. Black snakes are our friends on the farm. Hector, thank you for your help today."

She bent over and stroked Hector's glossy scales.

The other animals felt ashamed. They thought Hector was up to no good just because he was a snake.

42

"Thank you, Hector," said Puzzle.
"Thank you for saving my baby."
The kitten purred and nuzzled
Hector.

"Yes, thank you, Hector," said Mama
Hen.
The chicks peered from behind
their mother and peeped shyly.

43

"Thank you for helping me guard the barnyard," said
Sergeant Pepper.
"You're welcome. I just wanted to be a friend," said Hector.
"Then a friend you will be," said the kind rooster.

"Mother," Hector said as he sunned himself the next day with his new friends. "I've been looking for friends, and here they were all along in my own backyard.

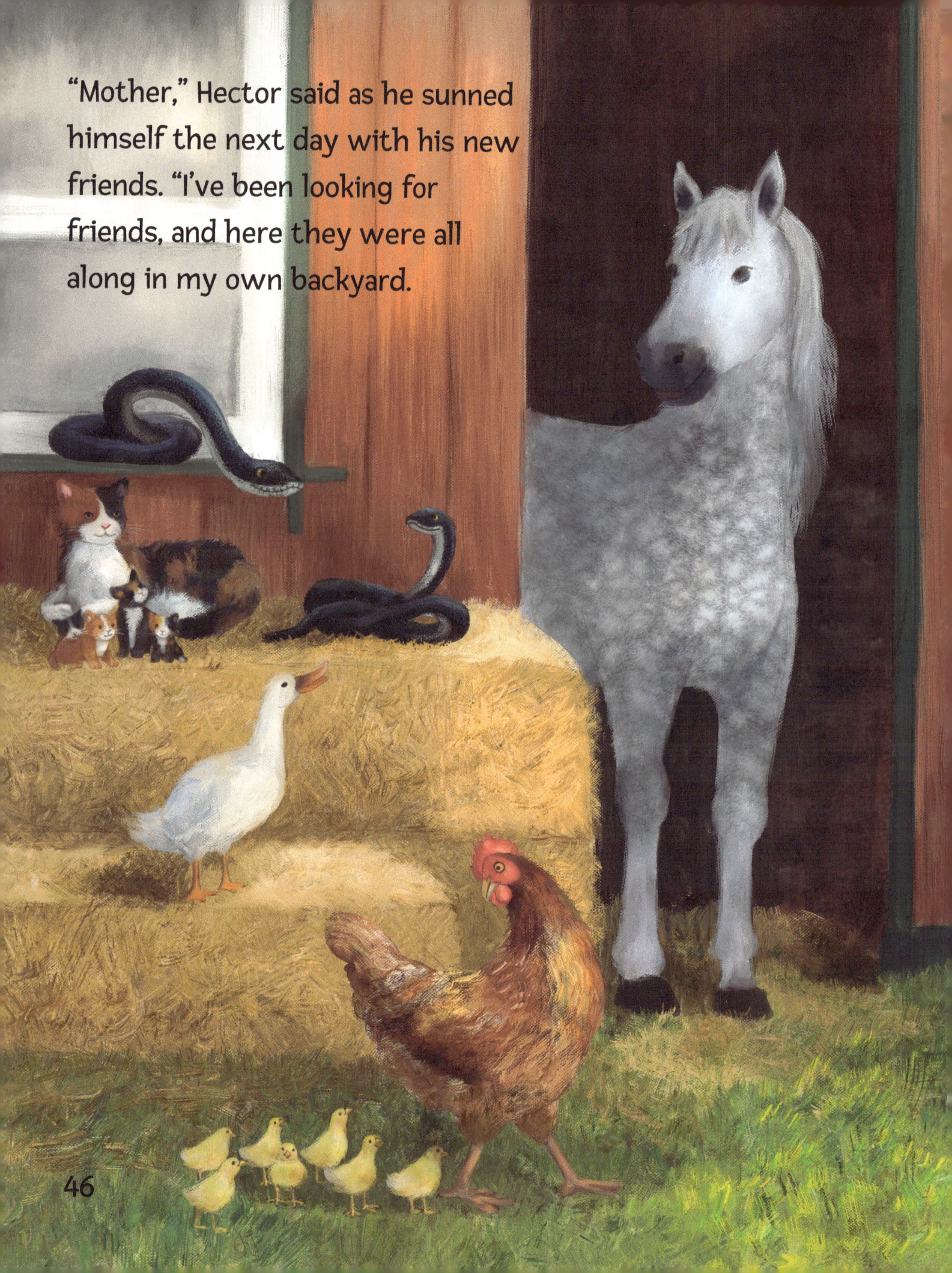

"We are so different, but now we are friends.
We only needed to talk to each other.
And I learned I just had to be myself
and not try to be somebody I am not.
Because real friends like you just
the way you are.